HEALERS

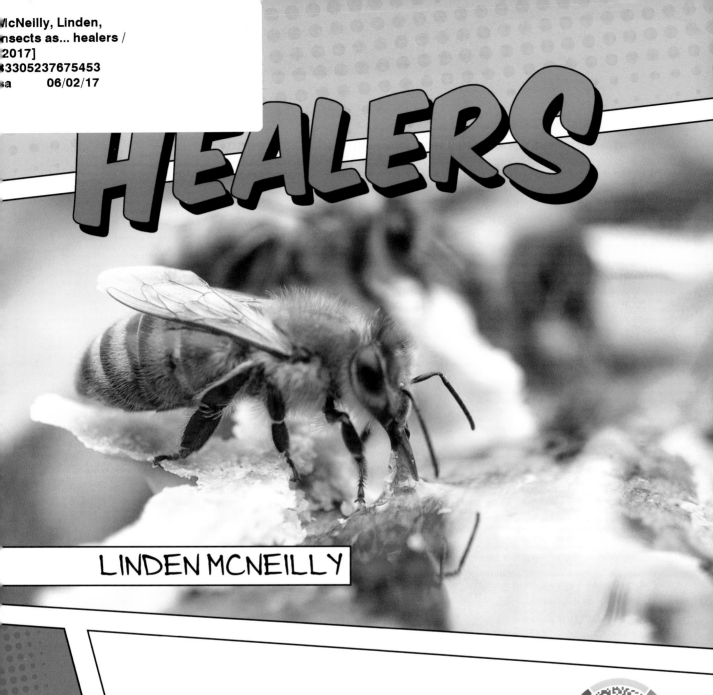

LINDEN MCNEILLY

Rourke
Educational Media

rourkeeducationalmedia.com

Scan for Related Titles
and Teacher Resources

Before Reading:

Building Academic Vocabulary and Background Knowledge

Before reading a book, it is important to tap into what your child or students already know about the topic. This will help them develop their vocabulary, increase their reading comprehension, and make connections across the curriculum.

1. *Look at the cover of the book. What will this book be about?*
2. *What do you already know about the topic?*
3. *Let's study the Table of Contents. What will you learn about in the book's chapters?*
4. *What would you like to learn about this topic? Do you think you might learn about it from this book? Why or why not?*
5. *Use a reading journal to write about your knowledge of this topic. Record what you already know about the topic and what you hope to learn about the topic.*
6. *Read the book.*
7. *In your reading journal, record what you learned about the topic and your response to the book.*
8. *After reading the book complete the activities below.*

Content Area Vocabulary
Use glossary words in a sentence.

biodegradable
compound
contaminate
extracted
immune
insulation
larvae
parasitic
toxin
venom

After Reading:

Comprehension and Extension Activity

After reading the book, work on the following questions with your child or students in order to check their level of reading comprehension and content mastery.

1. *Name three ways animals help humans. (Summarize)*
2. *What do scientists hope to use resilin for? (Infer)*
3. *What is propolis and what is it used for? (Asking questions)*
4. *When maggots eat dead tissue to expose healthy tissue, what is this process called? (Text to self connection)*
5. *How are bees being trained to sniff out bombs? (Asking questions)*

Extension Activity

Compare and Contrast! Draw two lines on a piece of paper to make three columns. Label the left column, "Insect Name." Label the middle, "Things in Common." Label the right side, "Differences." Using the book, write down every insect on the left side of the paper. After reading the book, list the things the insects have in common and their differences on your paper. What did you find? Were you surprised?

TABLE OF CONTENTS

CAN BUGS MAKE THIS BETTER?

Insects—those six-legged, antennae-waving creepy crawlers are all pests, right? Not so fast! Though insects can seem scream-worthy enough to run for the spray pesticide, hold the can.

Insects are helping humans in many ways. Whether in adult form—like bees, beetles or wasps—or the immature forms of **larvae** or worms, they can do wonders. They can be used to heal, give clues at crime scenes, sniff out explosives, and keep destructive pests from eating crops. They have so many special properties they offer endless opportunities for scientists to ask: Can bugs make this better?

THE BUZZ ON BEES

Did you know that honeybees gather more than nectar? They also collect tree resin, a sticky substance they bring back to the hive. Bees chew it and add beeswax, then coat the inside of their hive or shore up their honeycomb with it. Harvesters call it propolis, or bee glue.

A honeybee strengthens the honeycomb with propolis.

Propolis

Propolis has been used as medicine for several thousand years. It combats viral infections —like those that cause the flu and common cold—and **immune** diseases. Sometimes people put propolis directly on skin to clean and heal wounds or treat minor burns.

Bees sip nectar, digest it a little, and then pass it by mouth from bee to bee. The last bee vomits the liquid into the honeycomb. Their beating wings thicken it into honey. Beeswax seals it in.

7

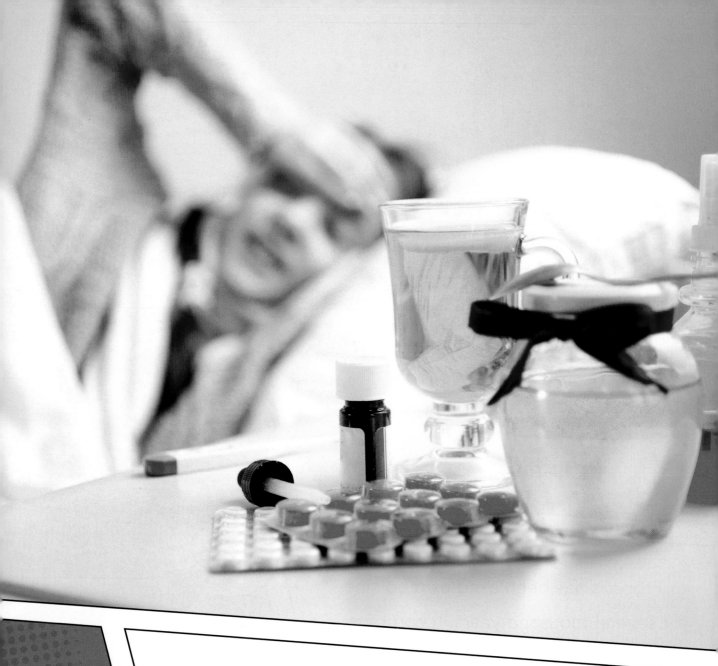

Honey is great for sweetening food, but it's also good for digestive problems. It's often added to hot drinks to soothe sore throats, colds and laryngitis. Honey has also been used to heal burns, rashes, and scar tissue.

Even bee stings have benefits. **Extracted** from the bee, or administered by stinging, bee **venom** has been used to reduce **inflammation**, which can help arthritis, rheumatism, and asthma. Scientists have also recently found that melittin, a **toxin** found in bee venom, is so tiny it can enter and destroy cells of the human immunodeficiency virus (HIV).

BAD BUGS DOING GOOD

The fall armyworm moth and its larvae have always been pests for crop farmers. But they might turn their reputation around as they provide hope for a faster growing flu vaccine.

Flu Virus

Hemagglutinin (HA)

Traditionally, flu vaccine manufacturing requires chicken eggs. Vaccine makers inject flu cells into millions of eggs and then wait up to three months for the virus to grow enough to provide vaccines. But cells from the ovaries of fall armyworms can reproduce using just the flu virus's outer coat instead of the whole virus, saving time—and lots of chicken eggs!

A tricky protein called hemagglutinin (HA) is a shape-shifter that flu viruses carry on their coats. It gets inside human cells and constantly changes, making every flu different.

IT'S A BIRD, IT'S A PLANE...
IT'S A GRASSHOPPER!

Have you ever watched a grasshopper jump many times the length of its body, or a fly beat its wings so many times it's too hard to see? An elastic protein inside their joints and wings called resilin helps insects repeatedly jump and fly without the aches and pains humans get from repetitive motions.

Scientists are extracting this protein from flies and mixing it with quick-growing bacteria to make new proteins. They hope to use this new resilin to repair human body parts such as vocal cords and heart valves.

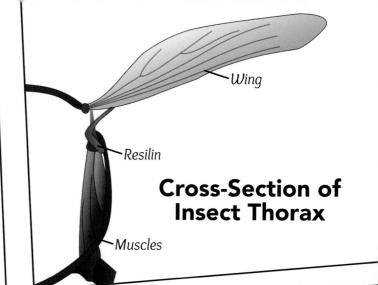

Wing

Resilin

Muscles

Cross-Section of Insect Thorax

A person who could jump like a grasshopper could clear a five-story building, or get from one end zone to the other on a football field in three jumps.

13

If a blister beetle landed on you and you smacked it, you'd get a cluster of blisters on your skin. These uncomfortable blisters would eventually disappear without medical treatment. So it may surprise you that a **compound** made with ground-up blister beetles is the main ingredient in some wart-removing products.

Blister beetles contain cantharidin, a toxic compound. Cantharidin uses its blistering magic on stubborn warts. When applied to warts, the compound makes blisters that help dissolve and pull away the wart. When the blisters disappear, so does the wart!

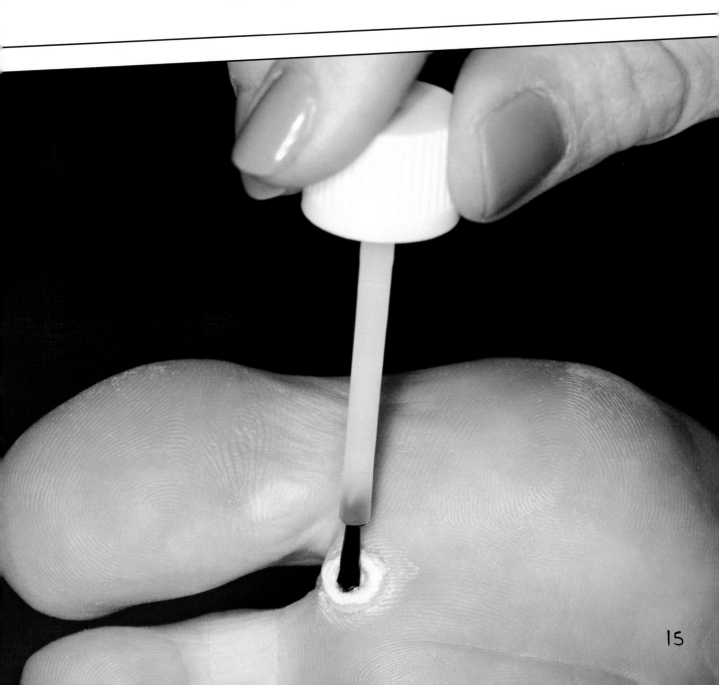

INSECTS THAT SAVE THE DAY

How would you like a squirming maggot in your wound? The thought of the little white wigglers feasting on your flesh might be disgusting, but they are wonderful helpers for doctors trying to heal open wounds without surgery.

Fly Life Cycle

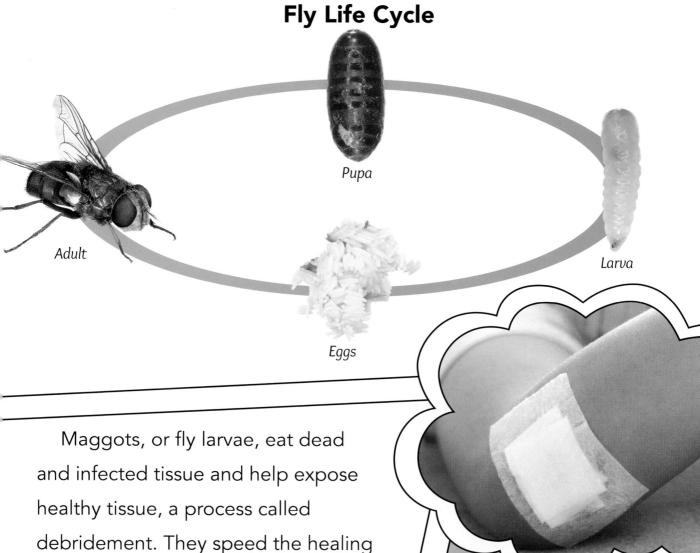

Pupa

Larva

Adult

Eggs

Maggots, or fly larvae, eat dead and infected tissue and help expose healthy tissue, a process called debridement. They speed the healing process by preventing clotting, so blood continues to flow, helping new tissue to grow. They can't stay forever, though. After a few days, they'll turn into flies, so they're removed and replaced with younger maggots.

Military surgeons have known for hundreds of years that soldiers with fly-infested wounds recovered more quickly than those without. But when antibiotics came along, most preferred the medication to maggots.

CUTTING POLLUTION WITH INSECTS

The world's problem with too much plastic may have an insect-based solution. Scientists have made a plastic from proteins in silk mixed with chemicals found in shrimp. It's made from the exoskeleton—the outside that crunches when you step on it. Even better, this plastic—unlike petroleum-based plastic—can adjust to the internal environment, protecting the contents from bacteria and mold.

Bug-based plastic is **biodegradable**, and since it's all natural, can actually enrich the soil after use. Scientists see other possible uses, like coverings for burns that dissolve over time, and medical sutures.

Silkworms eat mulberry leaves and then spin their cocoons of a single silk thread. To get the silk thread, the worms are boiled, and the thread unrolled carefully to keep it from breaking.

THE GOOD WASP

Gardeners and farmers often use pesticide to control the munching pests that destroy plants. But pesticides can run off into the soil and water, or **contaminate** the food you eat. Pesticides also kill helpful insects, making it possible for damaging ones to move in.

"Good bugs" like the tiny Trichogramma wasp can save the day.

This **parasitic** wasp doesn't harm plants. But its larvae can destroy the eggs of hundreds of species of leaf-eating moth and butterfly larvae. Trichogramma lays her own eggs inside the pest, which makes handy food for the larvae while destroying the garden pest.

The female Trichogramma wasp uses her antennae to measure the size of the egg. This measurement tells her how many of her own eggs to lay inside.

BUG DETECTIVES ON THE MOVE

Bees are being trained to sniff out hidden bombs. They are fed super sweet sugar water near soil packed with the chemicals found in explosives. The bees associate easy food with that smell. When they are near explosives, they stick out their proboscis in anticipation of the sweets they expect. Researchers keep the bees in tiny enclosed tubes so they can watch for the waving "tongue."

So far, they've helped Croatians detect land mines, or secretly buried explosive devices. They are being considered for use in detecting illegal drugs, too.

FIRST ON THE SCENE

Insects can help authorities solve deadly crimes. Because bodies go through different changes as they decompose, different species of insects are attracted at different times. This biological timeline gives forensic entomologists important information.

Blow flies are the first to arrive at a death scene. Their presence suggests that the death happened within days. But if they have had a chance to lay eggs, or the eggs have hatched into maggots, those are clues that more time has gone by. Beetles tell authorities that the death was even more distant, since their mouths only chew older, drier flesh.

Forensic detectives sometimes use cards with a life-sized photo of the insect on it, and information on its stages and habits to help at the scene of the crime.

NATURE'S THE BEST ENGINEER

Insects are the inspiration for tiny, all-seeing machines called microdrones. Watchful inventors studied actual fly movements and noticed how the exoskeleton crumpled neatly like an accordion to manage the impact of a collision.

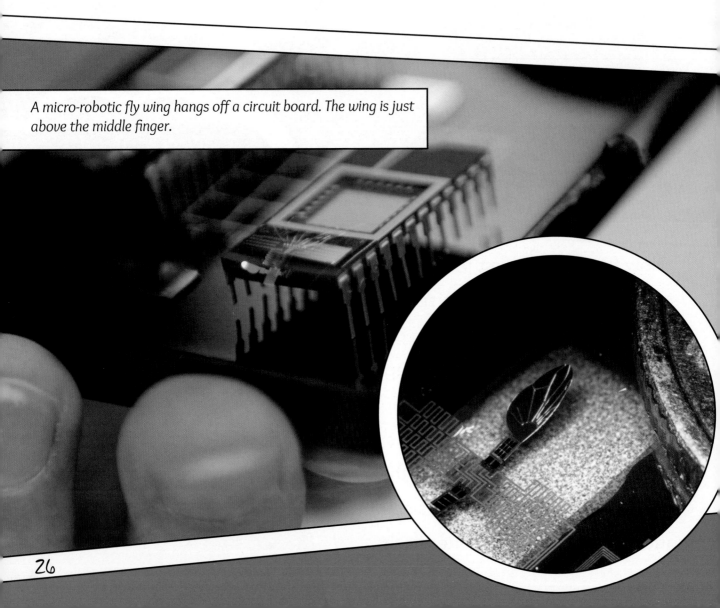

A micro-robotic fly wing hangs off a circuit board. The wing is just above the middle finger.

Modeled after flies, dragonflies, and bees, these little mechanical fliers mimic insects' bodies and wing movements to propel forward, fly in the wind, and recover from collisions. Regular drones don't do these things well; they break too easily.

Insects also use their wings to create their own wind—and this wind is what keeps them aloft.

The braconid wasp larvae act as parasites on the tomato hornworm.

Insects can help make the world work better. They eat pests, make plastic and rubber, provide healing power, and offer a blueprint to a tiny drone. They contribute to medicine and offer clues at the scene of a crime. They even push destructive bugs out so plants can grow!

Next time you see an insect, whether it's flying, crawling or wiggling, give it a closer look. You never know what secrets it holds for solving problems. Who knows, maybe an ant can be taught to do your homework!

GLOSSARY

biodegradable (bye-oh-di-GRAY-duh-buhl): able to be broken down by natural processes

compound (KAHM-pound): a substance, such as salt or water, that is made from two or more chemical elements

contaminate (kuhn-TAM-uh-nate): make harmful or undesirable

extracted (ek-STRAKT-id): removed or pulled out

immune (i-MYOON): if you are immune to a disease, you don't get sick from it

inflammation (in-fluh-MAY-shuhn): redness, swelling, heat, and pain, usually caused by an infection or injury

larvae (LAHR-vee): insects at the stage of development between egg and pupa, when they look like a worm

parasitic (par-uh-SIT-ik): an animal or plant that lives on or inside another animal or plant, taking nutrients from it

toxin (TAHK-sin): poison

venom (VEN-uhm): poison produced by bites or stings

INDEX

SHOW WHAT YOU KNOW

1. List three helpful things about bees in the areas of science or medicine.
2. How have studying bug movements helped scientists to design new technology?
3. How did early doctors know that blow flies were helpful?
4. List three insects that are usually considered pests that can do helpful things.
5. How do insects help detectives solve deadly crimes?

WEBSITES TO VISIT

www.nwf.org/Kids/Ranger-Rick/Animals/Insects-and-Arthropods

www.kidsgardening.org/node/11528

www.planetnatural.com/beneficial-insects-101/

ABOUT THE AUTHOR

Linden K. McNeilly is a writer who taught public school for many years. She loves to make handmade books and write stories. She co-wrote *Map Art Lab*, a book about maps and art. She lives in the redwoods in the Central Coast of California with her family. Find her at www.lindenmcneilly.com.

www.rourkeeducationalmedia.com

PHOTO CREDITS: Cover: © Tobias Zehndbauer, vblinov; Page 1: © Darios; Page 3: © Bonnie Taylor Barry; Page 4: © Nattawut Sottivilaipong; Page 5: © Josef Sowa, Solodov Alexey, Schantz, Aleksey Stemmer; Page 6: © Tischenko Irina; Page 7 © Auhustsinovich, StudioSmart; Page 8: © kryzhov; Page 9: © Darios, USBFCO; Page 10: © afnr, Elliotte Rusty Harold; Page 11: © Sean Locke Photography, Designua; Page 12: © Majo1122331; Page 13: © Wikipedia - Bugboy52.40, Artit Fongfung, Pressmaster, winui; Page 14: © kurt_G; Page 15: © Pavel L. Photo and Video; Page 16: © glebTv; Page 17: © Protasav AN, Swanpan Photography; Page 18: © Noppharat46; Page 19: © Falcona, snvv; Page 20: © PiggingFoto; Page 21: © National Science Foundation, Sue Robinson; Page 22: © kingfisher; Page 23: © Vadim Ivanov; Page 24: © MR. PHAKORN KAEWICHIT; Page 25: © dedek, Couperfield; Page 26: © US ARMY; Page 27: © US ARMY, Raid Khalil; Page 28: © Elizabeth O. Weller; Page 29: © Nato_Ost

Edited by: Keli Sipperley
Cover and Interior design by: Tara Raymo *www.creativelytara.com*

Library of Congress PCN Data

Insects as Healers / Linden K. McNeilly
(Insects As …)
ISBN (hard cover)(alk. paper) 978-1-68191-691-0
ISBN (soft cover) 978-1-68191-792-4
ISBN (e-Book) 978-1-68191-890-7
Library of Congress Control Number: 2016932567

Printed in the United States of America, North Mankato, Minnesota

Also Available as:

ROURKE'S e-Books